Lyn Marshall's
YOGA
FOR YOUR
CHILDREN

D1396563

SCHOCKEN BOOKS · NEW YORK

First published by SCHOCKEN BOOKS 1979

**Library of Congress Cataloging in
Publication Data**
Marshall, Lyn.
   Lyn Marshall's Yoga for your children.

   Includes index.
   SUMMARY: An introduction to the
philosophy and the basic positions of hatha
yoga.
   1. Yoga, Hatha—Juvenile literature.
2. Yoga, Hatha, for children. [1. Yoga] I.
Title: Yoga for your children.
RA781.7.M35   613.7   78–31344

Designed by Andrew Shoolbred
Photographs by Simon Farrell

Manufactured in Great Britain
Published in Great Britain by Ward Lock
Limited, London, a Pentos Company

Contents

Introduction

At last, I am delighted to present my book *Yoga for your Children*.

Since my first book *Wake up to Yoga* was published in 1975, I have been inundated with requests from children and parents alike for a special book on Yoga for children. The only thing that has prevented this was my lack of time. Now finally here it is, your children's complete, step by step Yoga practice guide.

I am particularly excited about this book because when I first began to practice Yoga, I used to wish it were possible for children to learn these easy, gentle, stretching movements that serve so well as either an alternative to the sports and P.E. generally taught in schools, or as a complementary way of moving the body, getting to the areas that sports and P.E. do not reach.

The movements are so simple, natural and easy to learn, that children of all ages will love to practice them. As you will see in the following pages, the Yoga movements are illustrated with many photographs and simple step-by-step instructions that children can follow on their own.

The movements all have easy to pronounce English names, and children find it very easy to remember them quickly.

Above all, the Yoga sessions are fun sessions. Children love to bend and stretch their bodies, and in my experience the few minutes spent practicing is never enough for them, they always want to continue. Just a few minutes of regular effortless practice will bring tremendous benefits to your children, and I believe that there is no better way of ensuring that your child improves and maintains his body in peak condition and establishes a pattern of self care and responsibility that he will retain for life.

I truly believe that this style of Yoga is the most perfect form of body movement and improvement that exists today, and it gives me great pleasure to be able to share it with you and your children.

Happy practicing,

Lyn

Note

This book is for you and your children.

Please read the first section thoroughly so that you can help and advise your child.

The second section of the book is written specifically for the children themselves, and you should either get them to read it completely or read it to them before you allow them to begin their practice.

What is this thing called Yoga?

At its simplest and most practical level, and as far as children are concerned, it is just a way of moving their bodies gently and without effort to improve and maintain them in tip-top condition. If, as your children get older, they develop an interest in the deeper meaning of Yoga, then I believe that they should be allowed to investigate further and decide for themselves if they would like to become more deeply involved in it. However, as far as this book is concerned, it has been designed to give children some very simple and safe basic movements which they can follow, enjoy and practice themselves, and which will improve and keep them in good condition from head to toe and set them up for life.

Where my style of Yoga differs

Many years ago some clever men devised positions of the body that would improve the physique and the workings of the internal organs and ensure that the body functioned at peak efficiency. These positions have become the classic Yoga postures and you may already have seen pictures of these in books. While these classic positions can be advantageous, I believe that it is better to take the body only as far as it will go naturally, rather than forcing it into a fixed pre-determined position, and it is on this basis that my style of Yoga was formed. Some of the positions I use were derived from these classic postures and others I have formulated myself. However, the main difference with my style of Yoga is that the body never over extends or stretches itself beyond its natural limit. By moving slowly and then stopping for a few seconds and holding a very comfortable position still, the body stretches at a natural pace, and there is never the possibility of straining or pulling muscles or ligaments. When adults are practicing the movements, the holding period is a count of five, for children it is a count of three. After holding the position for the count, which should be counted to yourself at approximately the same speed as seconds, the body returns to the starting position and then relaxes to allow the body to unwind before continuing. It is the way that these movements are executed **slowly and smoothly** that differentiates this style of Yoga from any other form of exercise or keep fit program, and the body's response, if treated gently this way, is really amazing. Strength and control begin to develop as soon as you begin to practice, and continues to build at a much quicker pace than by practicing other more energetic exercises. No strain is ever experienced and no **difficult** position ever attempted. Competition does not exist and the only important thing to remember is that each person must find his own comfortable holding position and stop and hold for the count there. If, for example, you and your child are practicing a movement together and he can only reach the knee while you can reach the lower calf, that is absolutely fine. As long as you are each going to your comfortable limit position and holding there for the count, then you are both getting an equal amount of benefit out of that movement. The next time that you do the same movement, you will find that you can go a little further, and so progress is gradual and positive.

Why this style of Yoga is so easy for children to practice and understand

My movements all have very easy names that children will memorize quickly and the names of the movements are very descriptive too. After practicing only once or twice, names like Body Roll, Push-Up and Squat will register in a child's mind and conjure up the body movement that it represents. Children seem to have a lot of fun doing the movements and use their imaginations. This is especially true with the animal movements like the Fish, Cobra, Cat and Lion. They really pretend that they are those animals and thoroughly enjoy imitating them.

In my experience, children lose interest immediately they are asked to do something they cannot do or are pushed too far. This method of doing the Yoga movements emphasizes emphatically that they need only go as far as their bodies go quite naturally, and consequently they enjoy it and never come to regard it as hard work.

Practice periods need be no more than a few minutes and most of the movements are repeated only twice, so there is no possibility of children becoming bored with the endless repetition and long practice sessions that normally accompany physical exercise.

There is no mysticism about this style of Yoga, or complicated and involved explanations. The movements are presented in an extremely simple manner, and the step-by-step instructions have been written especially for your children in a way that is easily understood, so that they can in fact practice alone.

Each movement is numbered very clearly for easy identification.

Your questions—and answers

What can my child expect to get out of Yoga?

Your child will first and foremost get a lot of pleasure out of just simply doing the movements. Children, as you know if you are a parent, love to bend and stretch and take great pleasure in moving as a form of self expression.

Your child can expect to strengthen and firm his body and limbs without overdeveloping the muscles, and to increase and maintain a high degree of suppleness and health right through the body.

Many children stand or sit badly and develop bad posture early on that becomes increasingly difficult to put right. Regular practice will correct this and eliminate the possibility of its recurring. It will also give your child an increased sense of balance and co-ordination.

Overweight is definitely a health hazard, and a fat child can easily become a fat adult. Also, we now know that a plump child is not necessarily a healthy one. Regular practice of these Yoga movements can safely reduce your child's weight by specifically moving and slimming that part of the body that is overweight, without cutting down on necessary protein or interfering in any way with the diet needed for growing bones and limbs.

Your child will develop a tremendous sense of body awareness as he executes the movements as instructed slowly and smoothly, and he will feel very acutely what it is like really to use the different joints and muscles in his body. Also, a degree of concentration is needed while doing the movements, which is completely different from when children are playing games or are involved in other forms of exercise, and their minds tend to be on everything and anything outside of their bodies. This brings about an internal awareness and in turn a sense of responsibility that carries over into adulthood; it is a feeling that the individual is totally responsible for his physical welfare and maintenance.

The fact that concentration is needed to do the movements definitely helps the child with his academic studies. A lot of children find it difficult to concentrate, and regular practice will increase their powers of concentration and allow them to take in much more information at school.

If your child is tense or nervous, regular practice of the movements will calm him down. Many children do get particularly tense at school exam time, and the practice of certain movements during the period just before exams has proved extremely valuable in dissolving these tensions. Receptivity increases, and your child becomes more aware of what is going on around him.

This is particularly noticeable when parents want their children to do something. It is not unusual to have to call your child repeatedly before he responds. Parents of children who practice Yoga say that they see a marked improvement in this area, that their children come first time when they are called and that they are much more alert than before. Once again, this increased receptivity will also be seen in their studies.

Unfortunately, many adults adopt the habit of shallow breathing and take in less than the maximum quantity of air with each breath. The deep breathing that is done with some of the movements, will teach your child to breathe automatically more correctly and set a precedent for life. It has also been known to help alleviate many breathing problems such as asthma and hay-fever.

Many parents have reported that shy children develop more self confidence and spontaneity and communicate much more freely with other children and with people around them generally.

Children of adolescent years may well find skin problems clearing up rapidly with regular practice.

Circulation will be improved right through the body.

Various medical disorders including those of a nervous origin, may be helped tremendously. (See page 12.)

But don't children get sufficient exercise in their normal day-to-day lives?

No, I don't believe that they do.

Children differ in terms of how active they are in an average day. I think that certainly many children do a lot of rushing around, but is this really exercise? Just how much of the body is being used and in what way? For example, it is essential, in order to have a healthy and supple back, that the back is fully flexed in both directions. That means really arching the back and then hollowing it out. Also, different parts of the body like the neck, arms and legs, need to be stretched and these limbs also need strengthening. Likewise, joints like ankles and wrists need regular attention or they can become weak, and there are very many other areas of a child's body that during the course of a rushing around day will not get any real attention. Yoga practice provides ideal insurance that your child is really moving and gently working every part of the body.

What age must my child be to start Yoga?

I would say that a good minimum age is between four and five years. Before that a child's attention will probably not stay on what he is doing for longer than a few seconds.

If your child is rather young, the best thing to do is to show him the book and then practice one or two of the movements with him. Alternatively, allow your child's natural inquisitiveness to lead him into Yoga by practicing yourself and then letting him join in with you.

Never force your child to practice, he will regard it as hard work and resent it. If he loses interest, fine, stop practicing for that day and try again the next day or a few days later.

If your child is very young, keep the practice time short to begin with, say four to five minutes only, and gradually increase it if your child is enjoying it. (See "How long should a practice session last?," page 14.)

There is no maximum age as far as this book is concerned, it is for small children, teenagers and adults alike. All ages will receive the tremendous benefits that regular practice will bring. Use the book to practice together as a family, or in a friendly group, or on your own if you prefer.

What difference is there between Yoga and the Sports and P.E. generally taught in school?

Yoga presents a complete alternative to the sports and P.E. generally taught in schools inasmuch as it is absolutely non-competitive. I have found that so many children feel inadequate or inferior if they do not do well at competitive sports, and this can lead to a turning off of interest in physical exercise generally. Yoga offers a totally different way of moving and enjoying one's body and it will instill a positive sense of well-being in a child. He doesn't have to win, and he can enjoy moving and stretching his body around and feeling good about it.

He will also develop a tremendous respect for how his body actually works, as he begins to feel individual joints and muscles as he is using them. This leads to a sense of responsibility and body awareness that children do not seem to get from games and sports.

Incidentally, I am delighted to note that more and more schools are now including Yoga in their curriculums.

Will Yoga interfere with my child's ability to do sports and games?

No, absolutely not, in fact Yoga often acts as a contributory factor by preparing the child's limbs and body so that at subsequent attempts at sports and games he will often excel.

Can Yoga do any harm?

If your child is fit and healthy and follows the instructions in the book, he will not do any harm to himself.

If your child is suffering from any medical condition or has a history of either physical or mental illness, then YOU MUST CHECK WITH YOUR DOCTOR FIRST before you allow him to begin to practice.

There are many instances where certain medical conditions can be greatly helped by regular practice, and more and more doctors are realizing this, so do not be afraid to go to your doctor for advice and, if necessary, show him this book so that he can see the kind of movements your child wishes to undertake.

There are also many conditions of a nervous origin that can be greatly helped by regular Yoga practice, and here again, I would urge you to discuss this with your doctor if your child is suffering from such a condition.

Caution

The movements in this book are specifically designed to be basic and safe, and will enable your child to practice regularly without doing himself any harm. It is true that many children can twist their bodies into far more complex positions than are shown here, but I believe that this can be extremely harmful for two reasons. First, a child may be able to get into complicated positions by virtue of his natural elasticity, but the strength and control that should accompany those positions will not have had time to develop, and a child could do himself immeasurable harm. Secondly, while bones and limbs are still growing, tremendous harm could be done if the body was continually put into advanced positions. I strongly recommend, therefore, that you should dissuade your child from attempting any Yoga postures other than the simple ones shown in this book.

Practice questions

Should I supervise my child or can he practice completely alone?

To begin with I think that you should supervise, especially with the very young ones. Check that your child is doing the movement according to the instructions and pictures in the book, and if he is not, correct him.

From the age of seven or older, when you think he knows the movements thoroughly, and subject to your feeling that he is responsible enough, it is perfectly all right for him to practice alone. Of course, all children differ and it is up to you to decide just when your child can practice unsupervised.

How long should a practice session last?

Only a few minutes at first. I recommend that your child begins with only one or two movements, but does them slowly and correctly. Then when he knows them you can add or interchange movements and gradually build up the practice time. Do not let him rush quickly through a lot of movements. He will be defeating the object and not receiving the benefits.

Must my child practice every day?

No, children as you are no doubt aware, periodically go off things, and it would be very wrong to force him to do his practice like school work every day. Encourage him to practice as often as he likes. That way you will find that his interest develops naturally and he will probably want to do more and more.

What time of the day should he practice?

He can practice at whatever time of the day he prefers, but before meals rather than after them—the stomach should have as little food in it as possible. Once your child is practicing regularly, it is a good idea to try to get him to stick to the same time of day for his practice session, as this will give him a sense of routine.

Which movements should I choose for him?

Always pick a good standing stretching movement to start with like the Triangle (No. 1) or Complete Breath (No. 2). Then a floor movement like the Cat (No. 8)—the important thing is to get a good balance by not doing movements that repeatedly exercise just one part of the body. For example, if you pick a movement that uses the shoulders and arms, then follow it with one that really stretches and strengthens the legs and so on. On page 60 you will find some practice routines that I have worked out for you of eight, fifteen and twenty minutes, and once your child has practiced for a while and knows the movements, you might like to try these. Your child will invariably develop favorite movements, and this is fine, but do not be afraid to interchange movements from time to time so that over a period of weeks he gets to do all the movements in the book.

What should my child wear to practice?

He or she should wear clothing that does not restrict movement in any way or the ability to breathe freely. This means nothing tight or restricting around the waist. The clothing worn by my young friends in this book is perfect for practice, leotards for the girls and elasticized trunks for the boys.

Does my child have to change his diet?

No, absolutely not. However, many adults do find, when they have been practicing for a while, that their tastes in food alter and they start to prefer less sugary and natural unadorned cleaner tasting foods. These changes, if they occur, can only be for the better, since cleaner and natural tasting food is generally much healthier.

I have an image of people doing Yoga who seem to become very introverted, passive and quiet, will my child become like that?

Practicing these movements regularly will not bring about any major changes in your child's character. However, you may notice some subtle changes. You may find, for example, that your child is becoming more obedient, more alert, more receptive to you, less restless and bored, more able to study, and more at ease with himself and life in general, and of course much fitter and healthier.

Section for children

Letter from Lyn

Dear Children,

First, I want to welcome you as my new Junior Students, and to tell you how happy I am that I can share this book with you.

I had so much fun writing and preparing the book with you in mind, and I know that you are really going to love doing the Yoga movements with me and my young friends on the following pages.

Many children have told me how much they like doing their Yoga practice together in a group with their friends, and you may like to try this too, or you can do it with your parents and brothers and sisters. Some children like to do their Yoga on their own. Whichever way you choose, I know that you will have a lot of fun doing the movements that have been specially selected for you.

On pages 22–23 you will find your T.T.T. or Top Ten Tips for all Junior Students. Read these at least twice or until you know them well before you begin to practice because they are very, very important. Try to remember your T.T.T. when you are actually doing the Yoga movements because they will really help you to do them correctly.

If there is anything at all that you do not understand, always ask your parents or a grown up, or, if you like, you can write to me and I shall be happy to help you.

With all my best wishes, and hoping that your Yoga practice will be, as it is for me, one of the most favorite things in your life.

Lyn Marshall

Meeting the children

I would like to introduce you to five young friends of mine, Clare, Stuart, Leigh, Robin and Jody, who helped me by practicing the movements with me, and I thought that you might like to know a little bit about them, so here they are.

Clare Nichola Wedgeworth is four and goes to nursery school. She also goes to ballet classes which she enjoys very much. She loves all animals, especially horses, and watches horse racing on the television whenever she can.

Clare has a little baby sister called Emma, and Clare loves to play with her and look after her as if she were her own little baby. However, Clare has decided that getting married and having children is really too much hard work.

This is the first time that Clare has done Yoga, and she really enjoys it.

Stuart Ross is five and has just started school and he has an older brother and sister. He loves football and swimming and reading Enid Blyton books.

Stuart likes going to school but sometimes he gets up to mischief. One day he hid all the other children's school books and then giggled while they looked everywhere for them. Another time when the school cat was licking her lips, Stuart decided that she was hungry, so he fed the goldfish to her. Of course the cat was very satisfied but the teacher very angry.

This is also the first time that Stuart has done Yoga.

Leigh Paget is ten, and she likes horse riding, and swimming and reading English history. She also likes to cook and help her mother around the house.

Leigh loves Yoga and has been practicing for about five years now. She started by practicing with her mother, but now does her practice session on her own when she gets in from school. She has her own practice mat and does a half an hour's practice every day.

Robin Lancelot Rix is eight and as you can see he has a very unusual middle name. Actually, Robin quite likes the name Lancelot because he happens to love English history, and especially the period of King Arthur and the knights of the Round Table.

Robin enjoys all sports, especially cricket and football. He also loves to play indoor games like backgammon, cards and chess.

Robin, like Clare and Stuart, had never done any Yoga before.

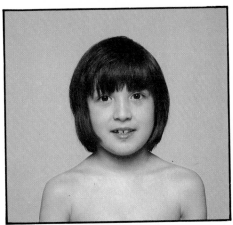

Jody Paget is five and is Leigh's sister. She is going to nursery school and really enjoys it, especially painting things.

Jody loves talking and if there is no one about, she will often have a conversation with herself.

Jody's favorite color is red and she is very proud of her red leotard which she wears to practice Yoga at home. She has been practicing Yoga for about a year now, but unlike her sister who practices alone, Jody still likes to practice with her mother.

Top Ten Tips for junior students

1 You MUST get your parents' permission first before you begin to practice.

2 Always do your Yoga practice before you have eaten a meal, and never after it, because this is very bad for your digestion, and you will not be able to do the movements correctly.

3 Wear clothes that are not tight, especially around your waist, and try to do your practice in a room that has carpet on the floor, or put a thick towel or a folded blanket on the floor.

4 When you are first starting, ask your parents to watch you to make sure that you are doing the movement correctly, then, if they allow you to, practice alone.

5 Only do two or three movements at the most to begin with, and really learn them well. Then, when you have been practicing them for a while and are really certain that you are doing them absolutely correctly, try a new movement if you want to. When you have been practicing for quite a while and know all the movements, if your parents agree, you can try the practice sessions on page 60.

6 Always do everything as SLOWLY and as SMOOTHLY as you possibly can, and the longer you take over each movement the better.

7 Do your Yoga in a quiet part of the house so that you can really concentrate on what you are doing.

8 Never ever rush because you want to do more movements when you are practicing. The golden rule is to do each movement really slowly and correctly and then relax as instructed before you start the next one.

9 For most of the movements, you have to stop in a comfortable position and hold that position absolutely still for a count of three. Count silently to yourself at the same speed as seconds, and then come out of the position and relax exactly as the instructions tell you.

10 Never ever push yourself to try to go further in any of the positions than is really comfortable. That means never feeling any strain or pain anywhere. If you do, immediately come out of the position and relax no matter what you are doing.

Now let's begin to practice.

1 Triangle

This is a good stretching movement. Do it to begin with as it really stretches your sides, legs and arms, and strengthens your back.

Keep your arms really wide open when you bend over and feel like an airplane in the sky.

Don't forget to move very slowly.

1 Stand with your legs and feet apart and your arms loosely hanging at your sides.

2 Breathe in deeply and raise your arms until they are level with your shoulders.

3 Slowly bend over to the right and grip your right leg firmly. Bring your left arm toward your ear.
Turn the palm of your hand to the floor.
Hold your position still for a count of three and breathe out slowly.

5 Breathe out as you bring your arms down to your sides and relax like this before you repeat over to your left.
Now repeat once again to each side.

4 Breathe in as you straighten up and come back to this position again.

6 After practicing for a while, you may be able to bend over a little further like Robin, with the top arm parallel to the floor.

2 Complete Breath

This is a deep breathing exercise that will really improve your breathing.

The arms go up and down to help you take in more air with each breath.

Look and see how the children's hands are. On the way up, in Picture 2, the hands are palms upward, and on the way down, in Picture 4, the palms are toward the floor. See if you can remember to do that.

1 Stand with your legs and feet together and your arms at your sides.

2 Now take a really deep breath and raise your arms up slowly.

3 Join your hands together right over your head.

4 Breathe out slowly as you bring your arms down. Now do it three more times.

3 Scissors

This movement will stretch your back and the backs of your legs and improve your balance.

This movement is called the Scissors because your arms should open and close at the same time just like a pair of scissors.

1 Stand with your feet slightly apart and your arms at your sides.

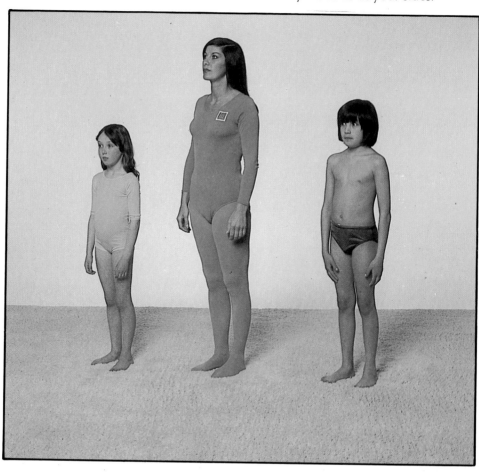

2 Breathe in deeply and bend forward, sliding your right hand down the inside of your right leg and raising your left arm and hand at the same time.
Look at your left hand.
Hold your position still for a count of three and slowly breathe out.

3 Breathe in as you slowly straighten your back and try to close your arms at the same speed so that they move together.

4 Breathe out as you relax like this. Then do the same thing on the other side.
Now repeat once again on each side.

Note
In Picture 2 Leigh has her head too low. You should have your head up a little more than that so that you can look over your shoulder at the back of your hand.

4 Body Roll

This rolling around movement is really good because it is one of the few movements that stretch and firm your waist. The Body Roll also helps you with your balance, and is fun to do.

Just breathe normally in and out while you are doing it.

1 Stand with your legs and feet together and your hands on your waist.

As you can see, Jody's feet are too far apart; they should be closer together.

2 Keeping your knees straight, bend forward from your waist.

3 Now roll slowly around to your right, stop and hold for a count of three.

4 Roll slowly around to the back, stop and hold for three.

5 Roll slowly around to your left, and hold your position for three.

6 Roll to the front again and then just let your arms and head relax like this.
Stand up straight and do the rolling movement around to your left.
Now do it once again in each direction.

5 Push-Up

The Push-Up makes your arms and
shoulders very strong and also your
wrists and hands, and it stretches the
backs of your legs too.

   Push your bottom right up as high
as you can when you do it.

   After you have taken a deep breath
in Picture 2, just breathe normally.

1 Get on your hands and knees
   and curl your toes under like Clare,
   Leigh and Robin.

2 Take a deep breath and push up and let your head hang right down. Hold your position still and count three.

3 Slowly lower your knees to the ground keeping them together. Wait a few seconds and then do it again.

Now relax like this for a few seconds.

6 Squat

This makes sure that your toe, ankle and knee joints are strong, and makes your leg muscles firm and it also helps you with your balance and posture.

Sometimes when you are starting to practice the Squat, it is hard to keep your balance, and you can see that Stuart in Picture 2 is losing his balance. If you concentrate it will really help you.

Clare is just beginning and she finds it hard to keep up on her toes in Picture 2, but with a little practice it will come.

Leigh's position in Picture 2 is perfect, so try to copy her.

1 Stand with your legs and feet together and raise your arms in front of you with your hands turned towards the floor. Breathe in deeply in this position.

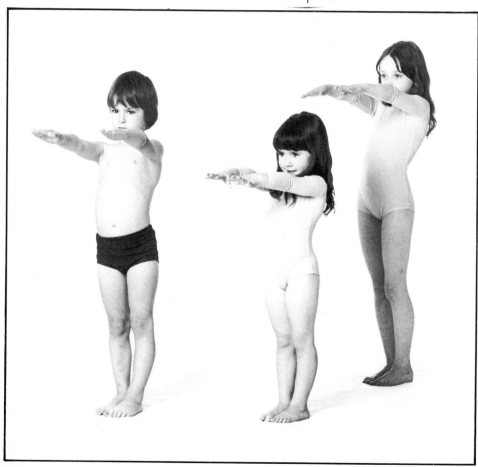

2 Keeping your knees together slowly bend them and try to keep your back straight. Breathe out.

3 Breathe in as you straighten your legs. Now do it another three times.

4 When you have done the Squat four times, relax like this for a few seconds.

7 Fish

This is one of my favorite movements, and I hope it will be one of yours.

Arch your back right up just like a fish, but try not to open your eyes or your mouth when you are doing it.

The Fish makes your back very supple and strong and really stretches the front of your neck. Just breathe normally in and out while you are doing the Fish.

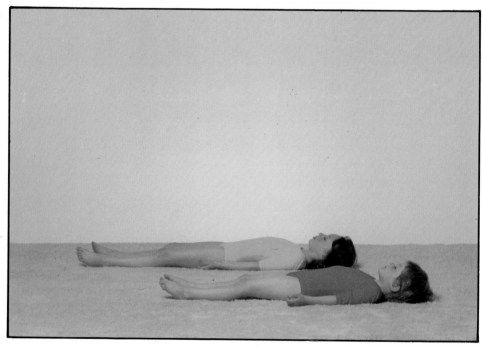

1 Start by completely relaxing like Jody and Leigh, with your eyes closed and your feet and hands relaxed.

2 Bring your legs and feet together
and make fists out of your hands
with your fingers in toward you.

3 Push down with your fists and arch
your back by pushing your chest up
and tilting your head backward.

Hold your position still for a count
of three.

4 Let your head slide back **slowly** and
then relax for a few seconds as in
Picture 1.

Now do the Fish again.

8 Cat

This is another favorite of mine because I love moving the way that a cat moves, really arching my spine up and down.

When you do it, imagine that you are a cat and enjoy stretching your back.

This also makes your arms, wrists and shoulders very strong.

Just breathe normally in and out when you are doing the Cat.

1 Get on your hands and knees like Stuart and Clare, then slowly make your back sink down and look up at the ceiling.
Hold your position for a count of three.

2 Now reverse your position slowly so that you really arch your back. Push your head down so that your chin is on your chest.

Hold it for a count of three.

3 Do the whole Cat movement once again, up and down, and then relax like this for a few seconds.

9 Coil

The Coil bends your back in completely the opposite direction to the Fish. Like the Fish it makes your back supple and strong, but this time it stretches the back of your neck.

Try to imagine that you are really coiling yourself up like a little ball when you do it.

Just breathe in and out normally for this one, and this time you can open your eyes.

1 Lie flat on the floor and bend your knees in to your chest with your knees together.

2 Loop your hands around your knees.

3 Carefully pull your knees in and bring your head as close as you can to your knees.
Hold your position still for a count of three.

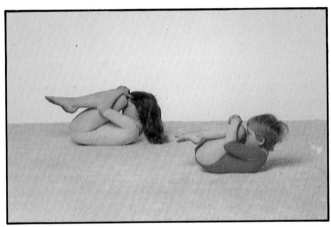

4 Slowly let your head go back on to the floor.
Wait a few seconds and do it again.
Now stretch your legs out and relax.

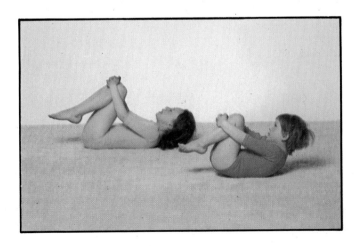

10 Cobra

The Cobra is a fantastic back bending movement, but be careful to do it very slowly and correctly.

If you have never done the Cobra before, then copy Robin in Picture 4. As you can see, his elbows are still a little bent. Jody has been doing the Cobra for a while now, and she can get her arms comfortably straight, see Picture 5. Try to keep your shoulders back and down when you do it, and your head back so that you can see the ceiling, and imagine how a Cobra really feels as it arches its back.

Breathe in and out normally while you are doing the Cobra.

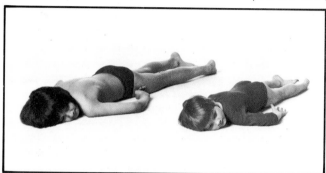

1 Lie on your tummy and relax exactly like Robin and Jody by bending your elbows and relaxing your fingers and feet.

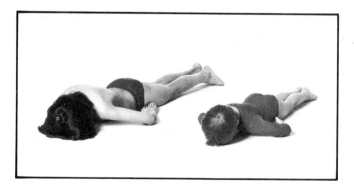

2 Bring your legs and feet close together and put your forehead flat on the floor.

3 Bring your hands underneath your shoulders with the palms of your hands toward the floor.

4 Push down with your hands and straighten your arms as much as you can comfortably.

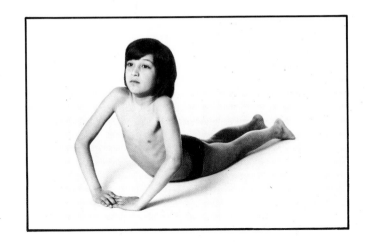

5 After practicing for a while you will be able to reach the position that Jody is in with her arms straight and her feet close together. Hold your position still for a count of three.

6 Slowly let your elbows bend so that you come down flat on the floor again, then go into position 1 and relax for a few seconds. Now do the Cobra once again.

11 Twist

You must really concentrate on my instructions with the Twist, otherwise you will get confused and use the wrong hand or leg.

You are actually using your body to make a lock and then twisting against it, to keep the center of your back supple and strong.

Breathe normally while you do the Twist.

1 Sit on the floor with both legs stretched out in front of you.

2 Cross your left leg over the right and put your left hand on the floor close to you exactly as Leigh and Robin are.

3 Now the slightly confusing part. With your right hand, grip the OUTSIDE of the right leg, but make absolutely sure that you have got the right position. See little picture.

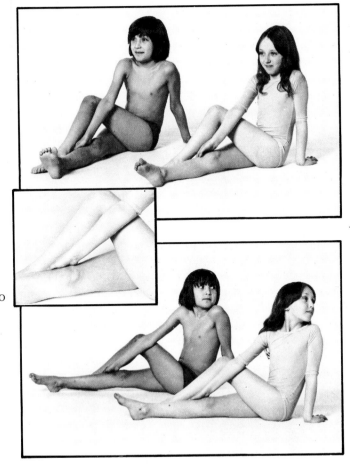

4 Twist slowly round to your left and look over your left shoulder. Hold your position for a count of three.
Turn round to the front and repeat.
Now do it twice on the other side.

12 Sit Up – Lie Down

You may think that sitting up and lying down is very simple, but we are going to do it very slowly and without using our hands. The Sit Up—Lie Down movement will strengthen all your muscles, especially your legs and tummy.

Breathe in and out normally.

1 Lie flat on the floor with your legs and feet together, and your arms at your sides.

2 Really make a big effort and reach forward with your arms and sit up. Try to do this slowly, without jerking.

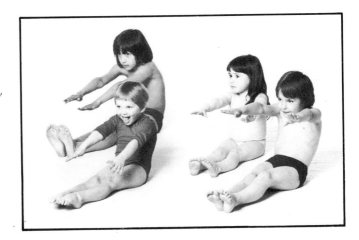

3 Bring your arms right up over your head.

4 Now see how slowly you can lie down, but push your toes down like Stuart and Clare and put your chin on your chest and you will find it easier. Sit up and lie down again another three times. Now lie and relax for a few seconds.

13 Leg Pull

This movement is really very good for
stretching and exercising each leg
separately.

1 Sit on the floor and stretch your
right leg out to the corner and bend
your left knee, bringing the foot in
close as we are doing here.

2 Raise your arms right above your head and take a deep breath.

3 Bring your arms down slowly.

4 Grip your leg, let your elbows bend and relax your head right over and breathe out. Hold your position for a count of three, then breathe in again as you come back to position 1. Repeat the movement once again and then change legs, and do it twice with the left leg stretched out.

14 Elbows

This is a good movement to do for your elbow joints and your arms.

This is one of the quick movements we do, so when you straighten your arms, do it sharply.

Check that your hands are in exactly the same position as ours in both pictures.

1 Bend your elbows and bring your hands in level with your chest. Make your hands into tight fists.

2 Sharply extend your arms with your hands still in fists. Do the movement again three more times.

15 Fingers

This is to exercise all your fingers one by one.

1 Grip the thumb of the left hand with the right hand and take a deep breath in. Pull both hands down slowly towards your tummy and breathe out.
Repeat it with all the fingers of the left hand and then change hands.

16 Side Bend

This is exactly what it says, a side bend that you do sitting down. You may find it a little difficult to balance at first as you bend over to the side, but with a little practice your balance will get better.

This really stretches your sides and makes your back very strong.

It is very easy to let your arms slip as you bend over as Jody and Stuart are doing in Picture 2, but try to keep your arms still if you can.

1 Sit on the floor with your legs crossed and your hands on your head.

2 Take a deep breath and slowly bend over to the right. Hold your position still for a count of three and breathe out.

3 Breathe in as you slowly straighten up and bend over to the other side. Hold it for a count of three and breathe out again.

4 Breathe in as you straighten your back up and then out again as you relax over like this. Now do it once again, to each side.

53

17 Head Roll

This is another one of my favorites because it is very relaxing to do.

Roll your head gently around very very slowly and when you know the movement, do it with your eyes closed.

This is a calming movement and it also stretches and makes your neck very strong.

1 Rest your hands on your knees and let your head relax forward.

2 Slowly roll your head around to your right, and stop there for a few seconds.

3 Slowly roll your head around to the back and stop there for a few seconds.

4 Slowly roll your head around to your left and stop there for a few seconds. Then come to the front again and roll your head around slowly in the other direction in the same way.

18 Lion

This one is fun. You can really imagine that you are a lion roaring.

So open your eyes very wide and stick your tongue out as far as you can.

Although this is a funny movement, it exercises your eyes, your tongue, your mouth and jaw, and your arms and fingers.

Try not to laugh too much while you are doing it the first time.

1 Sit with your legs crossed and your hands on your knees.

2 Spread your fingers wide, open your eyes as much as you can and push your tongue right out and down and make a Haaaaa sound as if you are a roaring lion. Hold it for three.

As you can see from this picture, Robin and Stuart lost their tongues somewhere along the way, so let's do it again.

3 Make your fingers wide, open your eyes, remember everyone's afraid of you, and push your tongue right out and down. That's better, I can see everyone's tongue this time. Hold it for a count of three.

Let your lion rest for a few seconds and do it again.

19 Foot Rotations

This is quite a funny movement because as you make your foot go round, your leg wants to go around as well. Don't let it; see if you can keep your leg still.

This movement keeps your toe joints and your ankle joints working well.

1 Raise one leg a few inches off the ground and slowly rotate the foot six times, then change legs and do it with the other foot.

Try to keep your knee straight.

Practice sessions

Practice sessions

Here are some practice sessions for eight, fifteen and twenty minutes.

After you have been practicing the different movements for a while and know them really thoroughly, ask your parents if you can begin these routines.

Whenever you do a practice session, you should always try to lie and relax in the Sleeping Pose, for a few minutes at the beginning and at the end of your session.

Start by doing one of the eight-minute Practice Sessions, and after a while, try the other eight-minute session. Later on, you can go on to the longer sessions if your parents agree.

You can change the movements in the sessions if you like later on, but make sure that you check in the index on page 63 first, to see what each movement does, and try to exercise as many different areas of your body as you can in each session.

Do not rush through your Practice Session. Do each movement slowly and correctly, and relax properly in between movements.

Do not worry if you take longer than the time that I have allowed here for each session. That is absolutely fine—remember, the slower you do the movements the better.

The Sleeping Pose
Always close your eyes when you do the Sleeping Pose and make sure that

you relax your legs, feet and hands exactly as in the picture.

Practice Sessions for 8 minutes

1 Sleeping pose
  Triangle (1)
  Cat (8)
  Sit Up – Lie Down (12)
  Sleeping pose

2 Sleeping pose
  Complete Breath (2)
  Squat (6)
  Cobra (10)
  Sleeping pose

Practice Sessions for 15 minutes

1 Sleeping pose
  Scissors (3)
  Fish (7)
  Coil (9)
  Leg Pull (13)
  Head Roll (17)
  Sleeping pose

2 Sleeping pose
  Body Roll (4)
  Push-Up (5)
  Twist (11)
  Elbows (14)
  Fingers (15)
  Foot Rotations (19)
  Sleeping pose

Practice Sessions for 20 minutes

1 Sleeping pose
  Triangle (1)
  Scissors (3)
  Cobra (10)
  Push-Up (5)
  Side Bend (16)
  Leg Pull (13)
  Head Roll (17)
  Sleeping pose

2 Sleeping pose
  Complete Breath (2)
  Body Roll (4)
  Fish (7)
  Coil (9)
  Twist (11)
  Lion (18)
  Sit Up – Lie Down (12)
  Sleeping pose

The numbers in brackets are the movement numbers.

Index of movements

Triangle
To really stretch the sides of the body, the legs and the arms.

Complete Breath
To enable the lungs to function efficiently and to improve [the] breathing generally.

Scissors
To stretch the back and the backs of the legs and to greatly improve balance and co-ordination.

Body Roll
To slim, firm and exercise the waist and to improve balance.

Push-Up
To improve the complexion by inverting the head, increasing the blood flow to the head and face.
To improve circulation generally and to stretch the back and the backs of the legs.
To strengthen shoulders, arms and wrists, and feet.

Squat
To enable the knee, toe and ankle joints to function efficiently and to make them strong.

Fish
To greatly improve strength and suppleness throughout the spine and to stretch the neck and throat.
To develop the chest.

Cat
To make the spine supple in both directions and to firm buttock muscles. To strengthen the arms, hands, wrists and shoulders.

Coil
To trim and firm the buttocks and thighs and to curve and stretch the spine right up to the top of the neck.

Cobra
To greatly improve suppleness and strength throughout the spine and to strengthen shoulders, arms, wrists and neck.

Twist
To keep the center of the back supple and strong and to firm and trim the waist line.

Sit Up—Lie Down
To strengthen and firm the tummy, legs, thighs, bottom, hips and waist and to strengthen the back, shoulders, arms and neck.

Leg Pull
To strengthen and firm the legs and thighs.

Side Bend
To really stretch the sides of the body. To firm and trim the buttocks and thighs, and to strengthen the back.

Elbows

To enable the elbow joints to function efficiently and to make them strong, and to strengthen the arms.

Fingers

To work the finger joints, and to strengthen the back, shoulders, upper arms, forearms and wrists.
To develop the chest.

Lion

To exercise the eyes, tongue, jaw and facial muscles, and to stretch and .strengthen the arms and fingers.

Head Roll

To relax and calm you.
To stretch and strengthen the neck.

Foot Rotations

To eliminate any stiffness in the toes, feet and ankles and to ensure that the muscles and joints remain in good working order.